Faces and Phases

Faces and Phases

Marketa George

THREE PUBLISHING

Published by:
Three C Publishing
880 Glenwood Ave SE
Suite#3559
Atlanta, Georgia 30316

Copyright © 2023 Marketa George
Cover design by Danyel Pullen II
Interior text design by Tom Davis
Old Mountain Press
www.oldmp.com
ISBN: 979-8-9875809-3-6

Faces and Phases
All rights reserved. Except for brief excerpts used in reviews, no portion of this work may be reproduced or published without expressed written permission from the author or the author's agent.

First Edition
Printed and bound in the United States of America by Morris Publishing®
3212 East Highway 30
Kearney, NE 68847
1-800-650-7888
www.MorrisPublishing.com
10 9 8 7 6 5 4 3 2 1

Preface

Take a stroll in time with me and my many "Faces and Phases." This lyrical journey exposes my strengths, my weaknesses, my peaks, my valleys, my journey into recognizing, honoring, valuing, and inspiring me.

Let's get into it…

Dedication

This collection is dedicated to the one person who has loved me, encouraged me, and stood with me in all of my failures and triumphs. This person has held me down, reminded me of my greatness, and has always been on the mountain and in the valley with me. She has held my face through every phase. Who is this special person?

She is ME!

CONTENTS

My Desires For My Mate 3
For Me 5
Leave 7
If I Ever See You Again 11
Rampaging 13
Taking Chances With My Chance 15
Dear Mr. 19
I Can Still 21
For Years 23
If He Ain't 27
If My Dress Could Talk 29
I Used To Attract 31
My Old Crush 35
"His" Unspoken Expectations 37
"Her" Unspoken Expectations 39
Call it Back 45
You Are Enough 47
Souled 51
I'm Just an Old Love Letter 55
It's Working 57
Be Addicted 59
Early 63
Put Your Mouth On Me 65
Make Room 67

Meet the Poetess 69

Keta's Keys

"When knowledge, wisdom, understanding, and cultural freedom collides, power is the result. Now that's supreme!"

Marketa George ©
All Rights reserved © 2023

My Desires For My Mate:

God-Chaser who knows the word and will of God concerning his life
A man who understands love and who loves me...in real life
A protector at all times
A respectful man who understands the seriousness of all his actions.
A goal-oriented man who will motivate and encourage
A man who will make me his priority
A man who values commitment and is honorable

For Me

For me…
I have loved you since I first saw you.
I thought, "He is so handsome, adorable even, and with an insatiable sexual appetite, I was hooked.
I saw past your haves and your have nots.
While I admired every inch of you, I wondered about that scar on your face.
Who had hurt you? How? Why? When?
You were so sweet and kind toward me…in the beginning.
You knew God and I thought he had sent you to look after and protect me.
Little was I prepared for the tumultuous turn of events that would suffocate and destroy the love.
It was the lies, cheating, and the sporadic abuse for me.
It was the historical laundry list of lustfully, naked and unashamed women outside of me.
It was the sad and simple excuses for me.
It was the vindictive behaviors for me.
It was the blame game for me.
It was the inner imprisonment, the hold, and the invisible chains I struggled to break for me.
It was the fake smiles and the pain behind my eyes for me.
It was the prayers for change, not understanding that one has to desire to change in order to change for me.
It was the hundreds of broken promises for me.
It was the death of a seed and the burial of our vows for me.
It was the glimpse of freedom slipping from my grasp for me.
It was the tears and anxiety of my children for me.
But now…it is the peace for me.
It is the rock for me.
It is the many nights and soiled pillow cases that washed away my desire to exist with you for me.
It is the overcoming of trauma bonds and unhealthy addiction for me.
It was the survival for me.
But now, it is the Source in me…for me.

Leave

Morning Sis
I want to put in a prayer request between You, me, and God.
I wake up many mornings bleeding inside from what appears
   to be a broken heart.
This anguish, this uncertainty, these questions, this disdain,
Misspoken vows, no hope, all lies, his inability to maintain
I do not trust this process,
I agonizingly stumble to find my peace
I know the word. I believe the word. This pain, this trauma,
   my soul can't keep
I try to bring my thoughts under submission,
I'm crying out from no damn vision.
I need clarity to relieve this pain,
I need the sun to outshine this rain.
Please pray that Source will guide me through,
In order to do what I must do, and that is,
Leave

Keta's Keys

"Struggle turns to strength, fear turns to faith, love leads the way. Living turns to legacy."

Marketa George ©
All Rights Reserved © 2023

If I Ever See You Again

If I ever see you again
I'd tell you how you changed my life
I'd tell you how I loved you hard despite my spiritual insights
I'd tell you how I thought our love would conquer a multitude
I'd tell you how I tricked myself into believing you were that dude
I'd tell you how I doubted myself and cried from inhaling the release
I'd tell you through the pain of your exit I finally am at peace

Rampaging

Healing is not pretty and it's not popular.
When a wound heals, it's at its ugliest.
You don't wanna look at it or touch it, but you must
    acknowledge it and take care of it.
I never meant to disobey the laws of attraction.
I thought I was doing what was right and honorable.
Too much of me and not enough Source.
I'm not mad at him, he was my casualty and I was his.
My tears are more potent than they've ever been and they
    flow like a river.
We all make mistakes, give too much and require too little.
Next time, I'll pay attention to the inner signals.
I'll judge you based on me.
I'll stay and play, or decide to stray based on my inner
    workings.
Yep…that's my move because it's my move.

Taking Chances With My Chance

Taking chances with my chance
    is like the devil in disguise
I took a chance with my chance
    and it yielded my demise
You took a chance with my chance
    and lost your damn mind
Another chance…
With a flashlight…
You will not find

Keta's Keys

"Some days will cause you to nurse yourself back to life. Some days will cause you to lay hands on yourself and speak life into your dry bones. Some days will cause you to be braver than you thought you could ever be. You got this."

Marketa George ©
All Rights Reserved © 2023

Dear Mr.

Dear Mr.
I hope this message finds you well.
I'm sure you are living your best life with zero regrets.
Now that this chapter of our lives has come to an end, I
    realize there were many lessons I had
to learn as a woman of God in order to get to a place of
    wisdom and peace.
I give part of that credit to you.
I had no clue how strong I was until strength was all I had.

Sincerely, Ms.

I Can Still

I can still love you
And want the best for you
Still care for you
And what you're going through
Stay away from you
Because of your super glue
It gets runny, then sticky
I become the fool
Fools for Love in the end
And know they never win
Sucked in
Fucked in
Now the game begins
But the healed stay the healed
Because they understand
Not your looks, not your sex
Will lock them down again
I can message you
Just to say a simple, "Hi "
Pure intentions
No convictions
Just like that
Bye ✌

For Years

For Years
For years I've been loved in a million wrong ways
By the wrong man or the wrong job
They inevitably could not stay
For years I have settled
For less than my worth
Depleted by "fake love"
And my feet hurt from that never ending search
For peace, for clarity, for a sense of myself
While sacrificing my time, my energy, my health and my wealth
Until that Sunday I woke up and desired something new
Something real, something right, something raw, something true
I got up, I looked up, and questioned what that could be
I flipped the switch, got really close,
And looked at me staring back at me.

Keta's Keys

"Stay focused Sis. Whatever is behind you deserves Zero (0) attention."

Marketa George ©
Rights Reserved © 2023

If He Ain't

If He Ain't…
A family man who knows where Source placed him in the household
An honest man who believes in truth
A vulnerable man who's not afraid to be open about his pain
A creating man with a provider's mentality, and generous with everything
A man who has learned to bring his thoughts and his actions under captivity
A man who controls his anger, especially when I can't
A man who honors his own mental well-being
A man who celebrates his manhood
I don't want him…PERIOD!

If My Dress Could Talk

I am the essence of evolution.
If my dress could talk
She'd tell a mighty story of
Struggle
Pain
Sadness
Loneliness
Healing
Deliverance
Victory
Self-love
Peace
Acceptance
If my dress could talk
She'd tell you she's the same dress…
I'm a different "G"

I Used To Attract

I used to attract
Father figures
Chaotically triggered
Complacently complicated men
The types that break
The types that bruise
Those were my top chosen
I did not know
I could not see
How I hurt them
How they hurt me
To every man who has ever loved me the best way you could
Thank you
To every man who impacted my spirit and stole my heart
Thank you
To the hims of the world who did not have the capacity to maintain, sustain, or retain me
Thank you
You raised me
Changed me
Dissolved me
Repurposed me
I found me
Unleashed me
I loved me
Bequeathed me
Thank you
Nah, I Thank Me!

Keta's Keys

"Magic happens when my house is still. Peace intoxicates me, and invades my space. This is when my magic happens."

Marketa George ©
All Rights Reserved © 2023

My Old Crush

"Oh hey, how have you been?"
"I'm Good, what about you?"
"It's so good to see you."
"It's good to see you too!"
Oh hell, he's still got it
My teenage hormones rush right through
I had never seen a more beautiful, and deliciously, graced face
Young and dangerous, tall and handsome, old memories I can't erase.
30 years of wrinkles in time, that boy has turned into a man.
30 years of missed romance, I guess we'll settle for being two old friends.
"Well listen, it's good to see you, take care of yourself."
Like an old, dust-filled book, I carefully put this teenage love back on the shelf.
My Old Crush

"His" Unspoken Expectations
Written by Anthony Clark

What is my unspoken expectation?
Girl please, I ain't got one, don't you remember?
I already told you what I wanted from you, when you were lying there sleeping, after a long day's work.
You heard me didn't you?
I thought you were cool, with giving me all of you, while you only get a piece of me.
I thought you said that you were cool, with letting me spend all of your hard earned money on my pipe dream?
I thought you'd be cool, with me slipping and sliding, while getting a little piece of pussy on the side.
You was supposed to forgive me, keep building with me, and not want to kill me for mismanaging your heart, fucking with mind, and scrambling your emotions that you let go of and lost, while trying to follow me and my indecisive, and double minded ways while being unstable in all of my thoughts.
James 1: 8.
But I thought you was cool with it.
I thought I could be smooth with it, as I had you and her and probably him and them to fulfill all my needs and wants.
But what did I need, what did I want?
I ain't even know, shit I was so broken, bruised and confused that all I wanted to do was use you, then confuse you, which ultimately was misusing you and your Love.
My unspoken expectations!

"Her" Unspoken Expectations

Unspoken Expectations
Oh I felt you loud and clear
Felt your heart, your pain, your fear
Night after night your heart was here
When your body would disappear
Time after time I began to notice
Day after day my inability to focus
Thinking and dreaming of my master plan
Inhaling the essence of this beautiful man
He was my king, only in my mind
The way we moved
Made the two of us shine
I wanted to be
Your everything
I wanted to have
A lifetime of dreams
Digging deep brought it out of me, You helped me transform my reality
You gave me what others couldn't comprehend
You gave me grace and space my friend
You made me smile and gave me joy
You did the same
I was girl
You were boy
And when the time came for intimacy
You gave
I gave
Gently
Generously
All this giving
All the takes
Surely, he's ready
Let's set a date
Were we ever really together?
Was this built to withstand forever?
What about

Same book?
What about
Same page?
I blame the Unspoken
For this God-forsaken place
Behind the scenes yielded detriment to vision;
Behind the mask you were plagued with indecision;
There you were, people pleasing us all
Catering
Serving
Down
Fall
You were torn between all of us
A matter of time before you'd combust
Figuring out which move to make
Costed a myriad of his/her mistakes
Then I'd run
You'd be close
Like a track star
Chasing gold
We grew dizzy
Changing lanes
You chased fame
I chased your name
Now in hindsight
In searching
Reflecting
There we both were
Deflecting
Neglecting
Going unheard
No voice
No clue
Too many
Compromises
You lost me
I lost you
Unspoken

Untrust
Unlove
Unjust
Expect
Defect
Suspect
Reject
SMH...Look at us

Keta's Keys

"Unspoken expectations lead to relationships on life support."

Marketa George ©
All Rights Reserved © 2023

Call it Back

Call it back
Last night
I heard the inner me calling my name
As I slept
I heard beginner me doing the same
Subconsciously
I awakened to hear their proclaims
Consciously
I pledge allegiance to my life reframed
First
I wept for the Girl that I used to be
Then
I wept for the Woman incubating in me
Now
I laugh with the Queen I am presently
By virtue
She is the free I am meant to be
Free to actualize
Audaciously
Vociferously
Unlimitedly
Continuously
Relentlessly
Unapologetically
Me

You Are Enough

I ain't never been
The "It "girl
The "Lit "girl
The "Split "girl
The " Bitch "girl
The "Pic "girl
The "Hot "girl
The "Thot "girl
I was always the:
Listener
Respectful
Loyal
Observant
Conservative
Aware
Urban
Royal
The world would have me believe that my different was beneath
That hard work, relentless focus, smart girl grind was all conceit.
I couldn't blend with the hood girls, always wasted, smoking weed
No tea and crumpets, pinky finger topics
For I was out of their league.
I was Two (2) parts hood and Three (3) parts good
An outcast to most
And always misunderstood
You see
The art of being you
Loving you
Embracing you
Are the key ingredients to a batter of peace and happiness, long overdue.
As we stumble through life
Unconsciously

Tripping over trash, debris, and mess
Let them carry opinions and perceptions
As for you…nevertheless
Let their negative be their negative
Let their stuff be their stuff
As for you keep loving you
Always remember
You are enough….

Souled

Source: thank you for renovating me.
I was that vacant spot
The corner lot
The block was hot
I was not
With broken glass
Filled with trash
And an emptiness so empty
Cars drove through and passed
My insides were crumbling
And dirt filled my space
My foundation was craving
No takers to trace
Then a visitor came
And opened me up
Appearance was rough
Yet, he noticed my good stuff
Examined my walls
Traveled my halls
He thought to himself
This ain't bad at all
He called in support
To get me straight
They came with their tools
For they knew by faith
They gutted my back
They gutted my front
They tore down the pieces
That hindered my stunt
They fixed my edges
They filled my cracks
They put me on the market
And just like that
I was good as new
I was ready to sell
No buyers remorse would come to derail

I was bought with a price
But first through death I died
Resuscitated, Rehabilitated
Approved...not denied
Souled.

Keta's Keys

"When your soul and spirit are at peace, that's happiness."

"Happiness is when the stuff that resides on the inside is unbothered and untethered."

Marketa George ©
All Rights Reserved © 2023

I'm Just an Old Love Letter

I'm just an old love letter
I've been floating around
Old and tattered
Ripped and scattered
Intended recipient
Not found
I'm just an old love letter
A sender searching for peace
I keep floating
Keep hoping
For relief and reprieve
Until I reach my destination
I'll continue to drift
Sailing
Gliding
Tossing
Turning
Through the winds
I shift
I'm just an old love letter
Without further ado
I'm just an old love letter
Four words
I still love you….♥

It's Working

It's Working
Do Not!
I repeat...
DO NOT!
Resort to feeling sorry for yourself again...
It's working!
Shame on them for walking away...
It's working!
You wrote the vision and the plan didn't pan...
It's working!
You took a risk and the liabilities almost took you out...
It's working!
You try to move, but this quicksand called life brings on more pressure to break free...
It's working!
What's working?
You're still here!
Learning
Growing
Glowing
Being
Delivering
Deliberating
Falling
Rising
Standing
Shuffling
Sticking
Moving
Creating
Manifesting
Expanding
Breathing
Breathing
Just breathe
Repeat after me...
"It's working!"

Be Addicted

Be addicted…
Be addicted to loving you
Be addicted to seeing you win
Be addicted to preserving your energy
Be addicted to saying no to the things that hinder you
Be addicted to walking ahead of the pack
Be addicted to having your own back
Be addicted to silently reflecting on your own progress
Be addicted to allowing those who can, do with and for you
Be addicted to sharpening saws
Be addicted to having your saw sharpened
Be addicted to honoring you
Simply put…Be addicted to you

Keta's Keys

"The day desire ignites your development, that's when elevation is created."

Marketa George ©
Rights Reserved © 2023

Early

As I lay in my bed, intentionally
Preparing for this remarkably unstoppable day
Electrical rain drops gush from heaven and my mind goes astray
Images of yesterday collide with today,
And whatever today will be
Mental escapades of future greatness staring, calling out to me
Thunder BOOMS.
Lightning STRIKES!
Mother Nature has her say
The rain pours,
My bed implores my body and begs it to just lay
I hear a faint sound kinda near,
But a distant, soft, sweet ring,
It jars my memory, wakes me gently, and steadies me from my-mid morning dreams
My rendezvous ends
As morning light bends
And I officially know it's time
To get up
Sit up
Re-up
Set up
And embrace this day as mine
Early

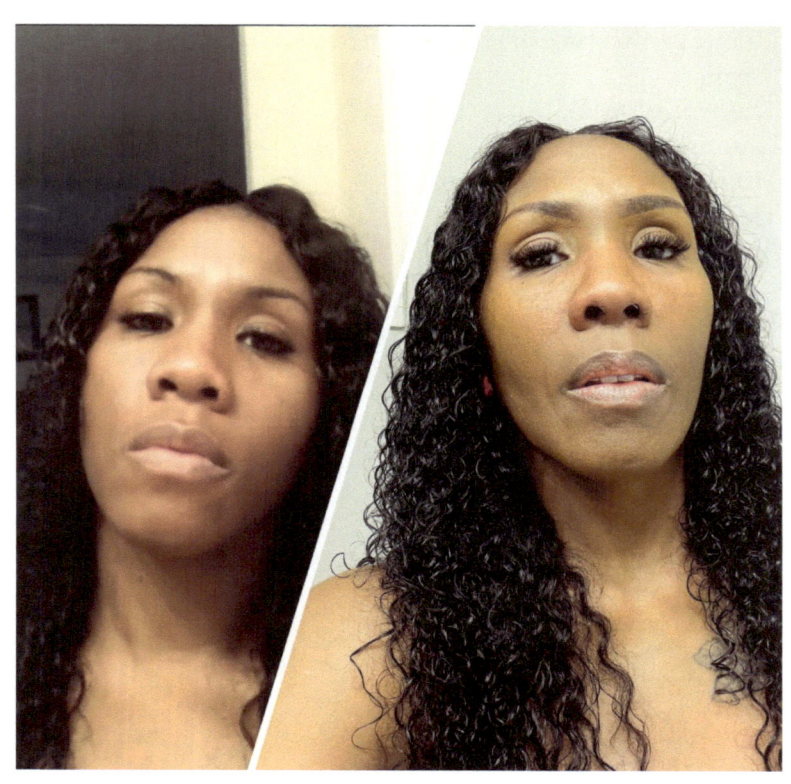

Put Your Mouth On Me

Put your mouth on me
If it's healthy
If it's healed
If it's whole
Let it tell me
Put your mouth on me
If your tongue speaks life
If your tongue can alter tudes
Taste strife
Spit life
Put your mouth on me
If it can change the game
It doesn't harm
It breathes love
It is a game change
Put your mouth on me
Full of style and grace
Bring peace
Sweet release
Come let me taste
Put your mouth on me
Let me kiss your lips
Translate
Motivate
Watch moods shift
Put your mouth on me
Let it elevate
Taste
Chew
Drink
Speak
Love
Vibrate
Put your mouth on me

Make Room

His presence overwhelms me
Grounds me
Contains me
Soothes me
Moves me
Behooves me
Tames me

His presence
Everlasting
Spell casting
Peace

His presence
Brings unfiltered
Effortless
Ease

His presence
Allows my softer side
To surface and be free
He
Stimulates and
Motivates me
His presence captivates me

His presence
Feels
Invincible
Incredible
Delectable

My mind is blown
My guard is gone
In his presence is where I belong

Make Room

Keta's Keys

"Small Minds Can't Have Big Visions."

Marketa George ©
All Rights Reserved © 2023

Meet the Poetess

MARKETA GEORGE is an Atlanta native, mother of three amazing children, Master educator of 23 years, Business woman, mentor, motivational speaker, fitness expert, and so much more. Follow her on social media @keta_theg

Here are more literary works from the publisher.

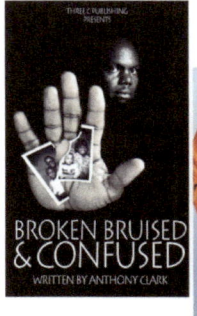

Get your copy today online at
www.oldmp/brokenbruisedandConfused
www.oldmp/the48lawsofthechaingang
www.oldmp/beautyforashes
www.threecpublishing.com
www.Amazon.com
www.barnesandnobles.com

www.ingramcontent.com/pod-product-compliance
Lightning Source LLC
Chambersburg PA
CBHW042332150426
43194CB00001B/30